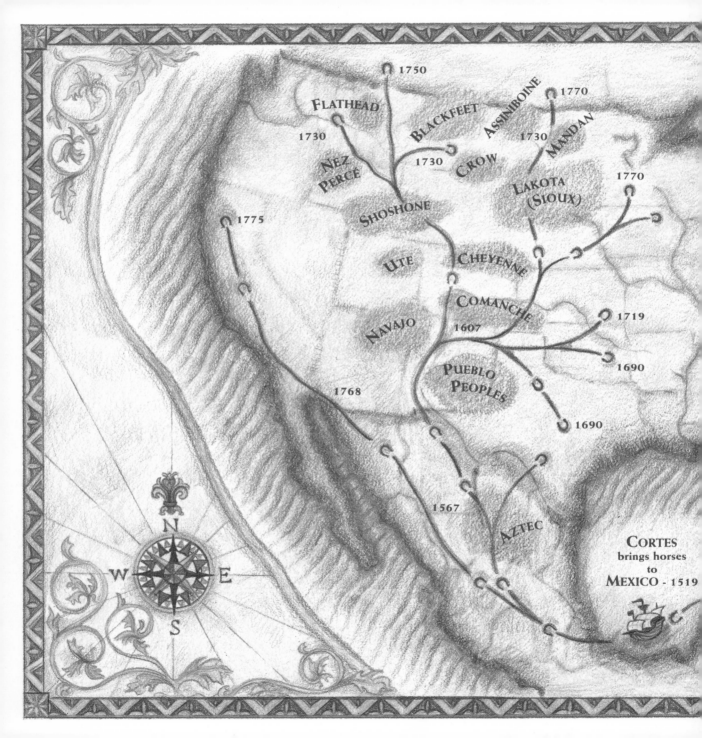

1750

FLATHEAD

BLACKFEET

ASSINIBOINE

1770

1730

NEZ PERCÉ

1730

CROW

1730

MANDAN

LAKOTA (SIOUX)

1770

SHOSHONE

1775

UTE

CHEYENNE

NAVAJO

COMANCHE

1719

1607

1690

PUEBLO PEOPLES

1768

1690

1567

AZTEC

CORTES
brings horses
to
MEXICO - 1519

N
W   E
S

HORSES

RETURN
TO
AMERICA

1511

CUBA

HISPANIOLA

1509

1526

1509

COLUMBUS
brings horses
from
SPAIN - 1493

After Columbus:
THE HORSE'S RETURN TO AMERICA

by Herman J. Viola

Illustrated by Deborah Howland

Soundprints

A Division of Trudy Management Corporation
Norwalk, Connecticut

*To American Indians everywhere,
especially those who share my love for the horse.*
— H.J.V.

*To my mother, who washed the dishes
so I could finish my work.*
— D.H.

Text copyright © 1992 by Viola Research Associates.
Book copyright © 1992 by Trudy Management Corporation,
165 Water Street, Norwalk, CT 06856, and Smithsonian Institution,
Washington, DC 20560.

Book Design: Johanna P. Shields

First Edition
10 9 8 7 6 5 4 3 2 1
Printed in Singapore

Library of Congress Cataloging-in-Publication Data

Viola, Herman J.

After Columbus : the horse's return to America / by Herman J. Viola ;
illustrated by Deborah Howland.
          p.   cm.
Summary: Discusses the reintroduction of the horse by Columbus, after its having
been extinct in North America for 8500 years, and how that animal changed forever
the lives of North Americans.
          ISBN 0-924483-61-X
1. Horses—America—Juvenile literature. [1. Indians of North America—Horses.
2. Horses. 3. Columbus, Christopher.] I. Howland, Deborah, ill. II. Title.
          SF284.A6V56   1992
          636.1'0097—dc20   92-11038
                                                                          AC

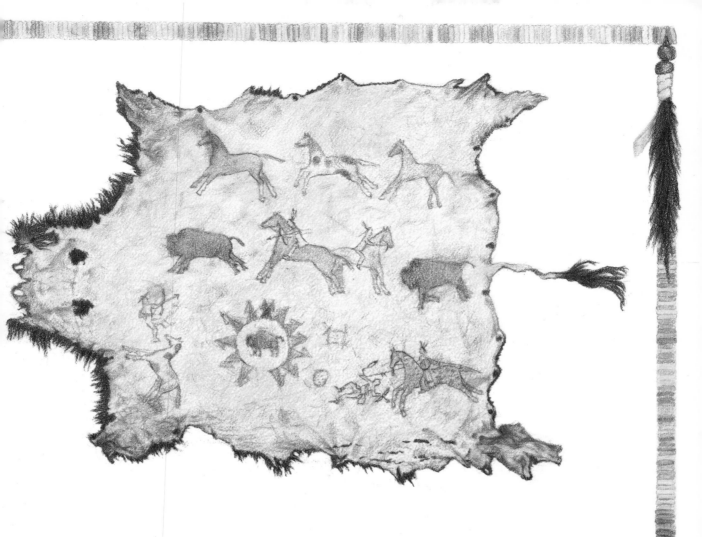

Out on the Great Plains, just east of the Rocky Mountains, the last horse in North America died 9,000 years ago. Why, then, are there horses in America today? Where did the horses ridden by the Indian tribes of the Great Plains come from? How did they get here? It was Christopher Columbus who brought horses back to America — just 500 years ago.

Columbus was a brave explorer from Genoa, a busy seaport in what is now the country of Italy. He was the son of a weaver, but he dreamed of a life at sea. He dreamed that one day he would be captain of his own ship. Then, he would sail to the mysterious Indies, far to the east, where he would trade for gold, spices and other valuable things. If he could do that he would become a wealthy and important person.

Columbus was sure that he could reach the Indies by sailing west. Many thought such a voyage impossible, but King Ferdinand and Queen Isabella of Spain believed Columbus might be right. An easier way to get to the Indies would help Spain, so the king and queen agreed to help Columbus. They provided three small sailing ships named the *Niña*, the *Pinta* and the *Santa Maria* for the voyage. Columbus's little fleet left Spain August 3, 1492, and sailed west beyond all lands known to Europeans.

1492 Columbus never found the Indies. On October 12, 1492, he did find land in the Caribbean Sea near what we now call North and South America — land that Europeans had known nothing about. Columbus was so sure that this land was part of the Indies that he called the people who lived there Indians.

After exploring many islands in the Caribbean Sea, Columbus set off in January 1493 to return to Spain so that he could report his exciting news to King Ferdinand and Queen Isabella. He brought with him parrots, gold ornaments and even some of the natives.

The news of Columbus's safe arrival in Spain in March 1493 and the stories of his wonderful discoveries delighted the people of Spain. Crowds along the streets cheered him. King Ferdinand and Queen Isabella were so thrilled by Columbus's stories and presents that they asked him to build a colony for Spain in the faraway land.

To start Spain's new colony, Columbus sailed west again in September 1493. Now he was in command of 17 ships, crowded with carpenters, farmers, soldiers and missionaries. Stowed on board the ships were all the tools and provisions that Columbus thought a new colony would need. Seeds and many different kinds of plants — wheat, barley and sugar cane — were on the ships so that they could be planted in the new colony. Animals came too: cows, pigs, chickens, goats, sheep — and, just as important, some horses for exploring this new land.

Taking horses to America on a sailing ship was not easy. The ships were very small and horses had no room to walk around. Often, horses had to ride in canvas slings that looked like hammocks.

Columbus built Spain's first colony in what he thought was the Indies on a large island that he named Hispaniola. The Arawak Indians who lived on this island in the Caribbean Sea feared Columbus's horses. They had never before seen an animal that could carry a person on its back. Some Indians called the horses "Sky Dogs," because they thought horses were very big dogs that came from heaven.

When Columbus saw that the Arawaks feared horses, he asked the king and queen to send him more. With horses, a few hundred Spaniards could protect their colony and control thousands of the Indians. Horses were needed, too, to help produce food on farms and to carry those Spaniards who seached for gold and spices. In fact, horses were so important to the new colony that very soon there were farms on Hispaniola just for raising horses.

1519 Columbus made his fourth and last voyage to the Americas in 1504. As the years passed, other Spaniards explored islands in the Caribbean Sea and started new colonies on some of them. Always, the Spaniards looked for gold and other precious things. They found little treasure on the islands, but heard stories from the natives of great wealth on the mainland — in a place called Mexico.

It was the Spanish conquistador Hernan Cortes who led 500 soldiers and sixteen horses into Mexico in 1519. Exploring inland, Cortez found great cities built by the Aztec Indians and ruled by a powerful king. In these cities, the Aztecs worshipped their gods in immense stone temples filled with treasures.

Aztecs were brave, and they had large armies — but no horses. The Aztecs were frightened by the Spaniards and their horses, but they fought very hard to protect their country. When the Spaniards defeated the Aztecs, they said that they owed their victory to their horses.

1670's Many years passed. Thanks to the horse, Spain now controlled most of South and Central America, Mexico and part of what is now the United States. One large settlement was named Santa Fe. Today Santa Fe is a city in the state of New Mexico. In the 17th century it was an outpost on the northern edge of the Spanish territories.

The Pueblo Indians lived near Santa Fe. Many of these peaceful natives worked for the Spaniards on large farms called missions. Mission priests taught the Pueblos about Christianity and showed them how to grow grapes and wheat and how to raise cows, sheep — and horses.

1680 The Pueblos cared for the horses, feeding them and giving them water. They made saddles and iron shoes for the horses. The Pueblos had no fear of horses and could do everything with them but ride or own them.

Tired of working for others and longing to practice their own religion, the Pueblos rebelled against the Spaniards in 1680. They chased the Spaniards from Santa Fe. Left behind were thousands of animals — including many horses.

The Pueblos did not keep all the horses for themselves. They traded some to their neighbors for valuable things such as blankets, baskets and furs. They taught their neighbors how to ride and care for horses.

Some of the Spanish horses escaped and became wild. In time, large herds of wild horses, or mustangs, roamed the open prairie lands of the West known as the Great Plains. Soon other Indians captured mustangs from these herds. They tamed and trained the mustangs and became fine riders.

Often an Indian family owned many horses, but a warrior usually had one that was special to him. It would be a beautiful, frisky horse — obedient, brave and swift. It was probably a spotted horse, called a pinto, because spotted horses were harder for enemies to see. A horse like this was a warrior's most valuable possession. To guard his best horse, he kept it near him at night. Sometimes he slept with one end of a rope tied to his wrist and the other end tied to this favorite horse.

For someone from another village to capture such a horse took great skill and bravery. An Indian boy was often willing to risk his life to take a valuable horse from an enemy tribe. Without making a sound, he would creep among the tepees of the enemy camp. If he found a tethered horse without waking up the village, he would cut the rope and lead the horse away as quietly as he could. When safely away from the village, he would mount the horse and race for home.

After risking his life for this valuable horse, the Indian boy might then give it away. That would show everyone in his village that he was as generous as he was brave.

By the year 1800, most natives of the American West had horses. Horses had changed their lives. Those whose way of life changed the most were the Arapaho, Cheyenne, Sioux and other tribes that lived on the Great Plains. These tribes are known as the Plains Indians.

Before they had horses, Plains Indians walked everywhere. On foot, they could not travel very fast or very far in one day, nor was it easy for them to hunt.

The Plains Indians hunted large animals called buffaloes. Hunting them were dangerous, and sometimes they were hard to find. When the hunt was successful, Indians had buffalo meat to eat and buffalo skins to make into blankets and covers for their homes — tents called tepees.

On horses, Plains Indians were able to travel far and fast. That helped them to find and follow buffalo herds. With horses to ride, the Plains Indians usually had plenty of meat to eat and enough animal skins to make clothing and tepees.

1860 Hunting on horseback took less time than hunting on foot. The Plains Indians now had more time to do other things they liked to do. They had more time to decorate things they used, such as their clothes, robes, and tepees. They could come together more often for visiting and trading, for games and celebrations. These were happy days for the Plains Indians.

American Indians of the Great Plains no longer live as they did in the 18th and 19th centuries. Even so, horses continue to be a treasured symbol of generosity, bravery, and freedom — traditions rooted in the past when North American Natives freed the horses at Santa Fe for everyone to have and to own.

About the Mustang

The mustang is a descendent of Andalusian horses brought from Spain to the Western Hemisphere by Columbus and the Spaniards who followed. After the 1680 Pueblo Indian revolt against the Spanish, horses that escaped formed wild herds on the Great Plains. These became prized mounts to those North American Natives bold and brave enough to capture them. Especially valued was the spotted mustang or pinto because of its natural camouflage.

Glossary

buffaloes: also called bison, are the largest land animals in North America. Both males and females have short, black horns, broad heads and massive bodies.

conquistador: a leader in the Spanish conquest of areas in the Americas, particularly Mexico and Peru.

giveaway: a ceremony during a gathering of American Indians at which valuable gifts are given away to others.

Indies: islands and mainland of eastern Asia from which spices and other valuable things could be obtained.

missionaries: those who travel to other lands to spread the practice of their own religion.

missions: the settlements of missionaries. Spanish missions of the 16th and 17th centuries were large farms.

prairie: relatively flat grassland with few trees.

tepees: cone-shaped tents made of animal skins supported by poles, used by the Plains Indians for shelter.

Points of Interest in this Book

p. 3 The border designs on several pages replicate quillwork of the Plains Indians. Quillwork is flattened and dyed porcupine quills sewn to clothes, bags, quivers, etc. as decoration.

pp. 8-9 Horses supported by hammocks. Their feet have been hobbled to prevent broken legs.

pp. 10-11 Border design is from Arawak wood carving and stone painting. Very little remains of Arawak art.

pp. 12-13 Border design from Aztec motifs.

pp. 14-15 Border design from Pueblo motifs. Indian wears loose, split to knee trousers introduced by the Spanish, as well as traditional breechcloth. He also wears sandals made from yucca plant fibers.

pp. 16-17 Border design is based on Pueblo motifs. A few Indians had secretly learned to ride as well as care for horses.

p. 18 Pueblos traded with Comanche neighbors to the north. Comanches wore lots of decoration (face, body and hair paint and jewelry), but simple, functional clothes.

pp. 20-21 The quillwork pattern used by Sioux Indians predated the use of beads for decoration. Leggings and shirts were often made of animal hides with the paws, tails, and legs left intact. The war bridle was made of braided buffalo hair.

pp. 22-23 The Sioux Indian raiding a Blackfoot camp wears no feathers or extra clothing which might make noise, nor does he wear any decoration that might catch the light.

pp. 24-25 The scout in the foreground uses a simple rawhide padded saddle with no stirrups. The saddle blanket is a doubled buffalo hide with hair left on.

pp. 26 The Sioux woman draws "thread" made of buffalo sinew through her mouth to keep it soft and moist in order to stitch animal hides together.

p. 27 The brave wears clothing made of flannel cloth obtained from the white man. The borders reflect the introduction of small "seed" beads in 1840. The smaller beads made possible more intricate, curved designs in a greater variety of colors.

pp. 28-29 Sioux dances often involve both men and women, who frequently dance separately from one another. Movement is usually reserved and dignified with men and women each having specific foot movements.

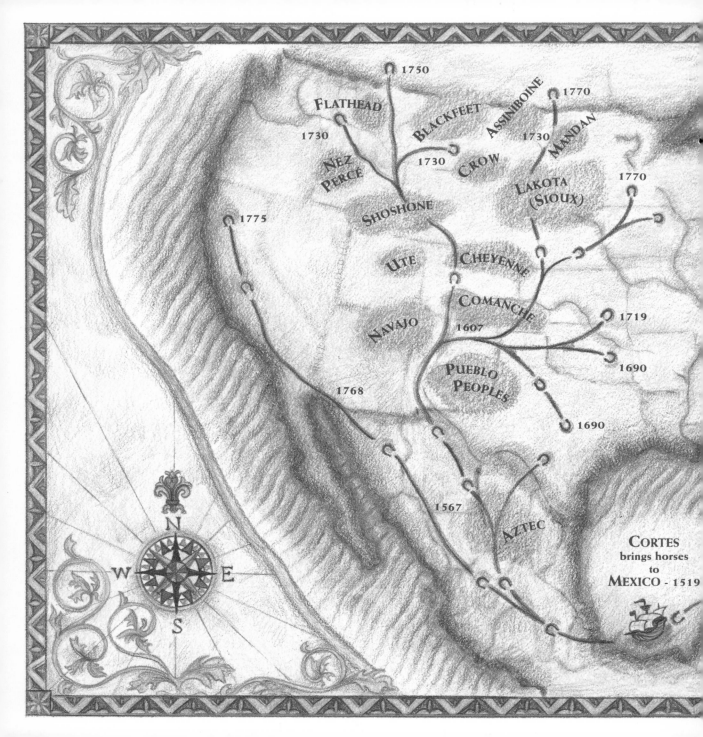

FLATHEAD

1730

NEZ PERCE

BLACKFEET

1730

CROW

ASSINIBOINE

1730

MANDAN

1750

1770

SHOSHONE

LAKOTA (SIOUX)

1770

1775

UTE

CHEYENNE

NAVAJO

COMANCHE

1607

PUEBLO PEOPLES

1719

1690

1768

1690

1567

AZTEC

CORTES
brings horses
to
MEXICO - 1519

N
W   E
S

·HORSES·

RETURN
TO
AMERICA

1511

CUBA

HISPANIOLA

1509

1526

1509

COLUMBUS
brings horses
from
SPAIN - 1493